My First Math Book

ARCTURUS

ARCTURUS

This edition published in 2018 by Arcturus Publishing Limited
26/27 Bickels Yard, 151–153 Bermondsey Street,
London SE1 3HA

Written by Paul Virr
Illustrated by Amanda Enright
Designed by Trudi Webb

ISBN: 978-1-78828-508-7
CH006084NT
Supplier 29, Date 0418, Print run 6462

Printed in China

How to use this book

Here are some helpful hints to help you solve the puzzles.

Useful Words

A "row" is a line of things placed side by side.

A "column" is a line going up and down.

If something is "symmetrical," one side becomes exactly like the other when you flip it.

Read the questions carefully to work out what you are being asked to do.

Always count slowly and steadily. Don't rush!

Parent's note:

This book is intended to support the learning your child does at school. You can help by encouraging your child to try all of the puzzles, even the ones they think may be difficult. Have a notebook handy so your child can write down their answers, or you may prefer to write directly into the book. Remember to have fun!

Counting Sheep

Little Bo Peep is counting her sheep! How many black sheep are there? How many white sheep? And how many sheep are there altogether?

Sharing Snacks

These children like to share. Can you give each child the same number of strawberries?

CHILLY CHALLENGE

Help this little penguin to get home as fast as she can. She can only step on the triangle-shaped icebergs!

Triangles have 3 sides.

START

HOME

6

Pizza Puzzle

Everyone's ordering pizza! Help the waiter work out how many slices to give each hungry customer.

Gone Fishing

Who has caught the most fish, the red team or the blue team? How many more fish did they catch than the losing team?

8

Happy Hens

Each happy hen lays eggs that match its feathers. Which hen has laid the most? How many eggs will the farmer collect?

Wacky Wheels

Everyone is whizzing about! How many wheels can you count? How many wheels would be left if all the scooters zoomed off home?

Spot Spotting

How many groups of bugs with the same number of spots can you find? Get out your magnifying glass, and take a closer look!

CIRCUS SHOW

Let's go to the circus! Which juggler is juggling numbers that add up to nine?

Apple Picking

Help the farmer to pick her apples.
How many red apples are there?
Are there more green apples or red apples?

Flower Finder

Just look at all these pretty flowers! How many flowers can you find that have six petals?

Cupcakes to Go!

Time for a tasty treat! If each child buys a different cupcake, which plate will have three cupcakes left?

Windy Day Fun

It's windy today—let's fly some kites! How many triangles can you see within each kite? It's more than four!

Triangles have three sides!

ON SAFARI

Can you spot three groups of three zebras? How many zebras is that?

There are four groups of two elephants. How many elephants can you spot?

Robot Factory

These shiny robots are ready to work together! Can you spot the robots that show an even number?

Frog Hopper

If every frog hops three lily pads down the page, which frog will land on lily pad number 6?

Road Racers

Add the numbers on the runners' tops. The team with the largest number wins the race! Which team will win?

Magic Key

Can you help the princess reach her friend? She has a magic key which unlocks doors that equal 12.

start

5+7

9+3

6+6

10+4

6+2

1+6

1+11

3+4

8+4

10+2

8+2

2+6

finish

SLEEPY KITTENS

The kittens are tired! They like to snuggle up with three kittens in a basket, so how many baskets would you need for all of them?

Flowerpot Fun

These rows of flowers make pretty patterns. Can you work out what flower to put in the last flowerpot in each row?

Toy Town

These children are playing with their wooden blocks. Can you see these shapes in the town? Which shape is not there?

Pirate Treasure!

Follow the arrows on the map to find Cap'n Redbeard's treasure. The numbers show you how many squares to move in each direction.

Blowing Bubbles

Bubbles, bubbles everywhere! How many groups of three can you spot?

Ski Run

Help this skier to find the best route down the mountain. She needs to ski through all the gates with odd numbers.

START

10

15

9

1

12

4

6

7

16

11

2

2

8

6

4

FINISH

14

HANGING OUT

What should you hang up next on each washing line to complete the pattern?

Crazy Cars

Work out the number of the car in the middle of each row by adding the numbers on the two cars either side.

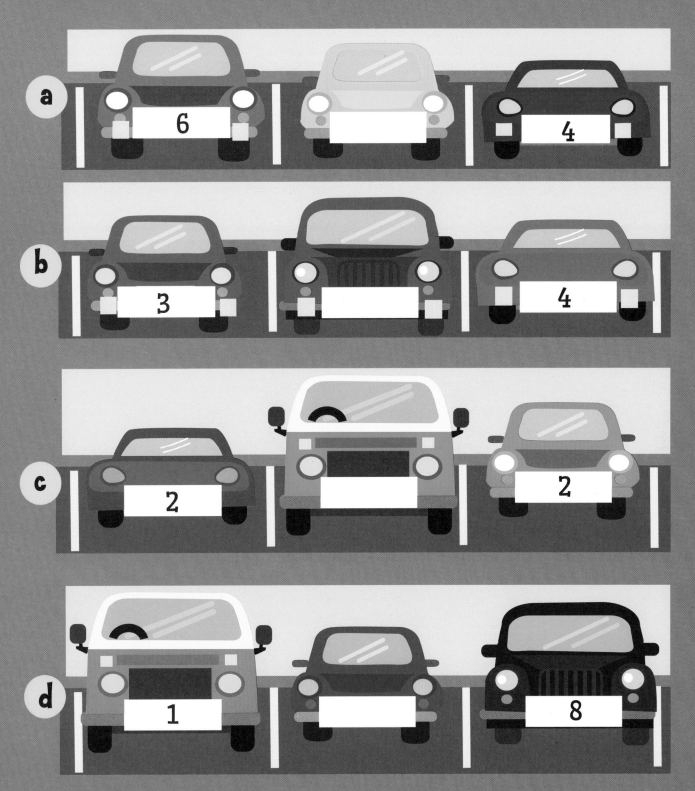

Fishy Fun

These happy fish are playing under the sea.
How many red fish are there? And how many blue fish?

How many orange and white fish can you see?

Spider Shapes

Sally Spider has made a lovely web. How many six-sided hexagons can you find? And how many triangles?

Number Crunching!

Big Bunny ate two carrots for lunch, but how many did his friends eat? Read the clues and work it out!

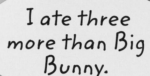

I ate three more than Big Bunny.

I ate as many carrots as Big Bunny and Red bunny together!

I ate one more than Big Bunny.

I ate half the amount that Big Bunny did.

Those two carrots were yummy!

Cleaning Windows

Each worker cleans the shape of window shown on their clothes. Which one cleans the most windows?

HOME SWEET HOME

These aliens have lost their way! Help them to find home. It's the planet with the most craters.

Butterfly Spotting

Look at the spots on the wings of these pretty butterflies. Which butterflies are symmetrical?

Symmetrical means they are the same on both sides.

Building Blocks

Look at the numbers on the square blocks. How do you make the number on the roof? Do you need to add or take away the numbers below?

a

7

3   4

b

5

8   3

c

3

9   6

d

9

2   7

e

6

1   5

38

Elves' Workshop

Can you help these busy elves? Spot the patterns, and work out what toy each elf should make next.

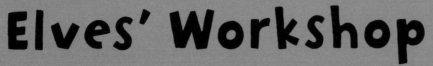

All Aboard!

This train is heading home. Its home is the shed with the lowest number. Where does it belong?

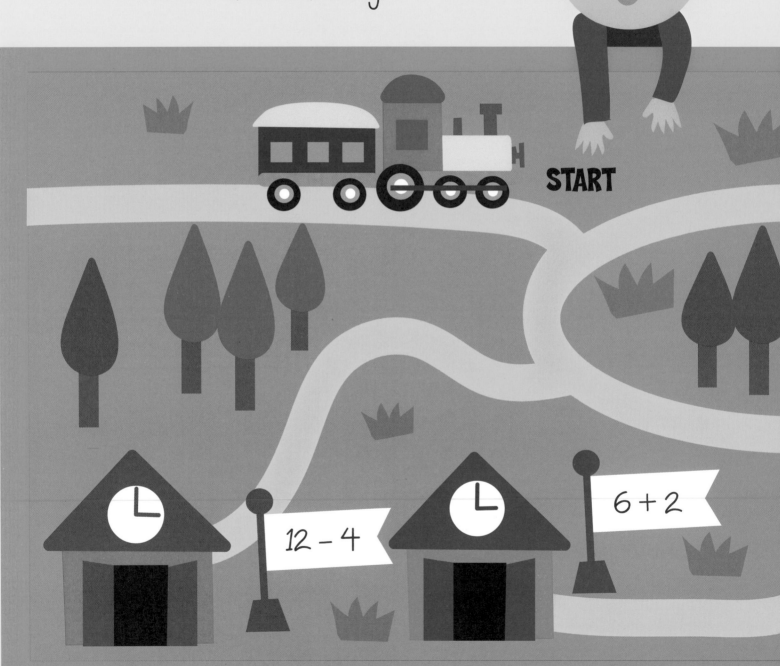

START

12 − 4

6 + 2

10 − 1

3 + 4

TRICK OR TREAT?

These friends have been given 15 chocolate chews. How many treats does each child get if they are shared out equally?

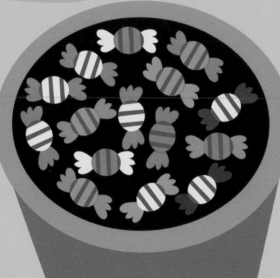

Sparkly Gems

Look at these sparkly bracelets! Which bracelet would give you the most points?

= 1 point

= 2 points

= 3 points

= 4 points

Moon Walk

Ready for blast off? Follow the arrows to reach your rocket safely. The numbers tell you how many squares to move in each direction.

Spy School

Welcome to Spy School! Crack the code to get to your class. You need the door with the code that equals 5.

Monkey Puzzle

Help this monkey to find her way home. Her tree is the one that equals 11.

18 − 7 = ?

20 − 7 = ?

14 − 7 = ?

15 − 7 = ?

19 − 7 = ?

Round Town

There are so many circles in Round Town! But how many wheels can you see?

DANCE MOVES

Pattern A

A dancer is missing from each of these groups. What move should that dancer be performing? Can you spot the patterns?

Pattern B

?

Going nuts!

Fluffytail squirrel wants to share her 18 acorns equally between her three kits. How many acorns do they each get?

Sunflower Sums

Pick the two sunflowers in each column that add up to 10.

Picnic Time

If there are 15 sandwiches and five children take two each, how many are left for later?

Happy Campers

How many tents can you see? How many shapes with 4 sides? How many with 3 sides?

FISHY FUN

Let's put all the fish into the big tank.
How many fish will be able to play together there?

Pumpkin Patch

Which face comes next in each row of Halloween pumpkins?

Busy Bees

Each bee visits a different flower before heading back to the hive. How many flowers are not visited by these bees?

Honey Hive

Who has made the most honey —
the red, orange, or yellow bees?

Silly Socks

The socks on the floor all have silly patterns,
but how many matching pairs can you find?
And how many odd socks?

Easy Cheese-y!

If each mouse eats the biggest piece of cheese on their plate, how many holes are left in the remaining two pieces?

LOOPY LOOPS

Which toy plane has looped
the loop the most times?

a b c d e

60

Crazy Castles

These children are drawing pictures of castles. Which castle contains the most square blocks?

Cool Cable Cars

The cable cars whizz up the mountain. Is the next cable car in each pattern spotty or stripey?

a

b

c

62

Chilly Penguins

Brrrr. These penguin parents have been knitting for their chicks. Can you match the parents to their chicks?

Costume Party

Let's dress up! What shape appears most on the costumes at this fun fashion show?

BUG HOTEL

How many circles can you spot? How many would be left if all the insects flew home?

Pumpkin Pie

Wooo! These little ghosts are hungry. Feed them with pumpkin pie! Is there any left for you?

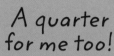

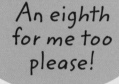

A quarter for me please.

A quarter for me too!

An eighth of pie please.

An eighth for me too please!

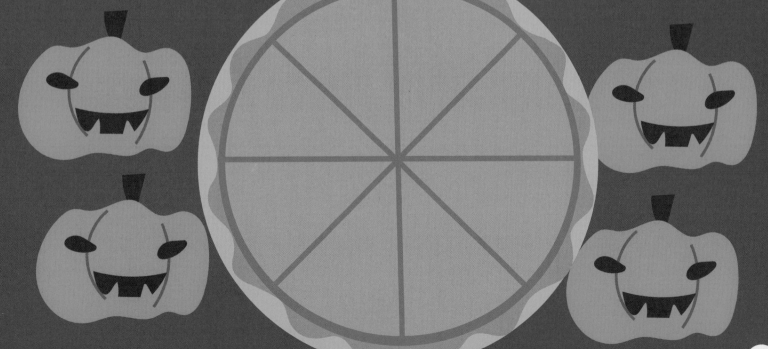

Happy Bunnies

If you give three more carrots to each bunny, which bunny will have 6 carrots for dinner?

Robot Workshop

These robots have been built from shapes.
How many shapes with four sides can
you spot in each robot?

a

b

c

Treasure Trail

Arrrr! Add up all the numbers to find out which pirate will score the most on their treasure trail.

PANCAKE PARTY

Chef has 18 eggs, and each of his giant pancakes needs 3 eggs. How many pancakes can he make?

Farmyard Fun

Farmer Brown has 12 sheep. If half go to the barn, and a quarter go to the fair, how many are left in the field?

number art

Help this artist by working out the missing number in each row.

a 4   6   8   ?   12

b 5   ?   15   20   25

c 3   6   ?   12   15

d 10   20   ?   40   50

Ice Cream!

Do more animals like chocolate or strawberry ice cream? How many ice creams are there altogether?

Plain Sailing!

It's a lovely day to sail a boat on the pond. How many triangles can you spot?

Ferris Wheel Fun

This Ferris wheel has 6 pods. If 12 children can ride it, how many fit equally into each pod?

TREAT TIME

It's treat time for these children. How many candy canes has Mr. Candy sold? And how many lollipops?

Bursting Balloons!

If this naughty bird pops two of each child's balloons, who will have 6 balloons left?

Car Rally

Vroom! Spot the counting patterns and work out the missing numbers.

a

10

20

30

b

5

10

20

c

3

6

9

Dog Show

What kind of dog comes next in each line at the dog show?

Sweet Dreams

It's bedtime for all sleepy children. Which blanket has the most spots?

Treasure Chest!

So much treasure, but only one key.
It fits the treasure chest that equals 4.

a $14 - 9 = ?$

b $5 - 3 = ?$

c $12 - 7 = ?$

d $15 - 9 = ?$

e $13 - 9 = ?$

HUNGRY MONSTERS

The Red Monster loves red food and the Green Monster loves green food. Who will eat the most at their monster picnic?

Shoe Shuffle

Everything is mixed up at the shoe store. How many matching pairs can you find?

Snowy Day

How many snowmen have the children made?
How many have hats? How many don't have hats?

Circus School

Find the missing numbers on the costumes of these circus acrobats, by adding the numbers from their friends below them.

Answers

Page 4 Counting Sheep

There are 4 black sheep, and 3 white sheep.
There are 7 sheep altogether.

Page 5 Sharing Snacks

Each child should have 3 strawberries.

Page 6 Chilly Challenge

Page 7 Pizza Puzzles

The first customer needs 2 slices.
The second customer needs 1 slice.
The third customer needs 4 slices.

Page 8 Gone Fishing

The red team has caught 11 fish, and the
blue team has caught 7 fish. The red team
has caught 4 more fish than the blue team.

Page 9 Happy Hens

The brown hen has laid 9 eggs, which
is the most. The farmer will collect 21 eggs.

Page 10 Wacky Wheels

There are 18 wheels in the picture.
There would be 8 wheels left if the
scooters zoomed home.

Page 11 Spot Spotting

There are 4 groups of bugs.

Page 12 Circus Show

Juggler b.

Page 13 Apple Picking

There are 10 red apples. There are more green apples than red apples.

Pages 14-15 Flower Finder

There are 6 flowers with 6 petals.

Page 16 Cupcakes to Go

Plate b.

Page 17 Windy Day Fun

There are 8 triangles within each kite

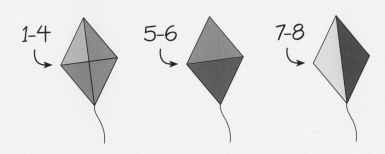

1-4   5-6   7-8

Pages 18-19 On Safari

There are 3 groups of 3 zebras., which is 9 zebras altogether. There are 8 elephants.

Page 20 Robot Factory

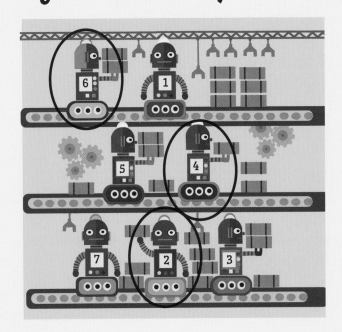

Page 21 Frog Hopper

Frog d.

Page 22 Road Racers

Red team = 14 points.

Blue team = 12 points.

Yellow team = 15 points.

Green team = 11 points.

The yellow team will win.

Page 23 Magic Key

Page 24 Sleepy Kittens

You would need 4 baskets for the kittens.

Page 25 Flowerpot Fun

Page 26 Toy Town

All the shapes appear, except the star.

Page 27 Pirate Treasure!

Page 28 Blowing Bubbles

There are 5 groups of 3 bubbles.

Page 29 Ski Run

Page 30 Hanging Out

Page 31 Crazy Cars

a = 10.

b = 7.

c = 4.

d = 9.

Page 32 Fishy Fun

There are 3 red fish, and 5 blue fish.
There are 7 orange and white fish.

Page 33 Spider Shapes

There are 3 hexagons, and 18 triangles.

Page 34 Number Crunching!

Black Bunny ate 5 carrots.

Red Bunny ate 3 carrots.

White Bunny ate 1 carrot.

Yellow Bunny ate 5 carrots.

Page 35 Cleaning Windows

The worker cleaning the square
windows cleans the most.

Page 36 Home Sweet Home

The green planet has the most craters.

Page 37 Butterfly Spotting

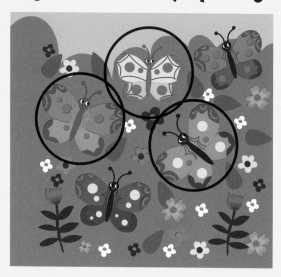

Page 38 Building Blocks

a Add 3 and 4 to equal 7.
b Take away 3 from 8 to equal 5.
c Take away 6 from 9 to equal 3.
d Add 2 and 7 to equal 9.
e Add 1 and 5 to equal 6.

Page 39 Elves' Workshop

Pages 40-41 All Aboard!

The train's home is the green shed.

Page 42 Trick or Treat

Each child gets 3 chocolate chews.

Page 43 Sparkly Gems

The bracelet with 4 triangles
would give you the most points.

Page 44 Moon Walk

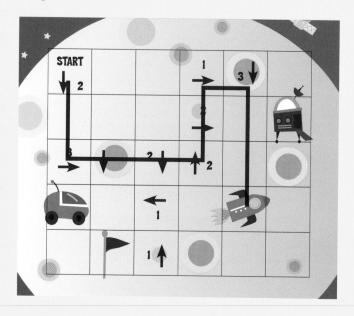

Page 45 Spy School

The green door adds up to 5

Page 46 Monkey Puzzle

Page 47 Round Town

There are 8 wheels in the picture.

Pages 48-49 Dance Moves

Page 50 Going Nuts!

They each get 6 acorns.

Page 51 Sunflower Sums

$a = 6 + 4$
$b = 3 + 7$
$c = 1 + 9$
$d = 5 + 5$
$e = 8 + 2$

Page 52 Picnic Time

There are 5 sandwiches for later.

Page 53 Happy Campers

There are 4 tents.
There are 4 shapes with 4 sides.
There are 6 shapes with 3 sides.

Page 54 Fishy Fun

13 fish will be able to play together.

Page 55 Pumpkin Patch

Page 56 Busy Bees

Three flowers are not visited.

Page 57 Honey Hive

The yellow bees have made most honey.

Page 58 Silly Socks

There are 10 pairs of socks, and two odd socks.

Page 59 Easy Cheese-y

a = 7 holes.
b = 7 holes.
c = 9 holes.

Page 60 Loopy Loops

Plane e.

Page 61 Crazy Castles

The orange castle.

Page 62 Cool Cable Cars

a = spots.
b = stripes.
c = stripes.

Page 63 Chilly Penguins

Group a has the scarves.
Group b has the gloves.
Group c has the hats.

Pages 64-65 Costume Party

Triangles.

Page 66 Bug Hotel

There are 25 circles.
There would be 9 circles if all the insects left.

Page 67 Pumpkin Pie

Yes, there are two slices left.

Page 68 Happy Bunnies

Bunny a.

Page 69 Robot Workshop

a = 9 shapes.
b = 11 shapes.
c = 8 shapes.

Pages 70-71 Treasure Trail

Pirate d.

Page 72 Pancake Party

6 pancakes.

Page 73 Farmyard Fun

6 sheep go to the barn, and 3 sheep go to the fair, so there are 3 sheep left.

Page 74 Number Art

Page 75 ice Cream!

There are 7 chocolate ice creams and 6 strawberry ice creams.
There are 13 ice creams altogether.

Page 76 Plain Sailing!

There are 13 triangles.

Page 77 Ferris Wheel Fun

2 children fit into each pod.

Page 78 Treat Time

Mr. Candy has sold 4 candy canes, and 7 lollipops.

Page 79 Bursting Balloons

Child a will have six balloons left if the bird pops two.

Page 80 Car Rally

a = 40

b = 15

c = 12

Page 81 Dog Show

Here are the missing dogs from each row.

Page 82 Sweet Dreams

Blanket b has the most spots.

Page 83 Treasure Chest

The key opens chest e.

Chest a = 5

Chest b = 2

Chest c = 5

Chest d = 6

Chest e = 4

Page 84 Hungry Monsters

The red monster eats the most.

Page 85 Shoe Shuffle

There are 9 matching pairs of shoes.

Page 86 Snowy Day

There are 9 snowmen.

7 have hats, and 2 do not have hats.

Page 87 Circus School

a = 40

b = 60

c = 30

d = 20